Religious Poems

Religious Poems

William F. Greene

Copyright © 2011 by William F. Greene.

Library of Congress Control Number: 2011905883
ISBN: Hardcover   978-1-4628-5664-0
             Softcover   978-1-4628-5663-3
             Ebook   978-1-4628-5665-7

To order additional copies of this book, contact:
Xlibris Corporation
1-888-795-4274
www.Xlibris.com
Orders@Xlibris.com
97092

A World Trade Center Story

I cried for a time, but no more,
For three days I lay buried.
those firemen and volunteers
who recovered my tattered form,
held me gently and proud they were.
The New York Port Authority,
my generous custodian,
loaned me for some openings like
The World Series and Superbowl,
yet, the sombre celebration
I joined in Kabul, Afghanistan,
among my American troops,
was a bit more heartfelt for me.
My crowning experience though,
was flying again at Ground Zero,
as the NYFD lifesavers
planted me firmly at the scene!
Yes, my feelings run deep and strong,
I am at home where I belong.
Out of retirement today,
circling the Olympic Stadium,
some billions watched my torn stripes,
which I hope help you to stay firm
for freedom's fight for why I fly.
I fly for the Olympic gold
in every American,
that their inner fire glows.
When I realized that my star field
in blue was intact, I rejoiced!
A paradigm for unity
still prevails as you coalesce
and strive for world peacefulness.
At seven by ten feet or so,
I safeguard this God blessed land,
hoping to fly for a long time.
In your sensitive care, I shall!

Scene at Salt Lake City Olympics
opening ceremony 8February 2002,
an inspiration for this poem.

**by William F. Greene, Cdr., USN
retired in 1974. Written 2-08-2002**

Religious poetry

These writings began shortly after I began writing poetry in 1987 in England at age 60 while my Christian attitudes and thinking matured some more. These characteristics appeared in my religious rhymes. I continued writing on many other topics as the ideas popped into my mind day or night. It was a new and rewarding experience for me to write of them. For several years I've wanted to compile a book such as this one and finally decided to just do it! The date written appears at the end of each poem enabling me to find it in a Dell WORD file. Also a reader is able to see my style and conviction development over time.

This work offered insight into my own faith and ability to translate it into terms that others can appreciate in their own faith journey. Many poems appeared in church monthly newsletters, some in a local newspaper. Along the way, I studied poetry in a local college evening course that prompted some variety in my work. If this book is Part I, a subsequent longer book, Part II, will contain Fun and Serious poems.

For two years as a Methodist Church lay visiting pastor, I've used this growth in faith in contacts with our church members unable to come to church. I find meaningful ideas and pictures to copy into a folded 5X8 inch personalized card for these people during frequent visits. At times, I include a poem. I play hymns on my Yamaha keyboard and provide communion to them as well each month. The rewards are substantial.

Even though I met Robert Frost in his Baker Library office at Dartmouth College in 1944, it was 43 years later, early in retirement and clear out of the blue, that I began writing in rhyme. In another five years, I'd honor Robert Frost with a poem! In this book, there are some Christmas Poems, one on a 9-11 World Trade Center Flag, a Canadian Adventure and others on experiences in Vermont, my wife's home state. Rhyming has been a pleasant way to record experiences in our world. I hope that you will enjoy these poems as much as I have in writing and publishing them.

William F. Greene
BS & MS in ME

CHRISTIAN POEMS
CONTENTS

TRIBUTE TO REV. DON BARNES

Rev. Don Barnes is a honey.
He's right on the money,
Disposition sunny!

In every sector
Where bees make their nectar,
Don is their director.

We have loved him for years
And sought him when in tears,
Only to leave with cheers.

He's taught us agape
—It's the Lord's sarape
And a fine canape.

While he's been off to school,
Don is nobody's fool-
He can be really cool.

Deacons love him a lot,
He gives all that he's got,
A counselor that's hot!

With great admiration,

—Marion and Bill Greene
in Palos Verdes, CA
27 October 1988

A BIRTHDAY GREETING

Thanksgiving's gone
Soon Christmas will be here,
It always brings us a lot of cheer!
Families, little tots and gifts endear,
Especially those that come by reindeer!

The prize is for those in each hemisphere,
Who believe in the Babe that we revere.
Wise men it's true, were drawn on that night clear,
From far-off lands and were sincere.

Frankincense and Myrrh—gifts of yesteryear,
Proclaimed our Lord's birth for the balladeer.
Mary and Joseph from that stable drear,
Were blessed by the Father, His Son to rear.

He proved bright, humble and would shed a tear,
For mankind and self when Romans did jeer.
Christ brought gentleness, love, respect, not fear,
His works are well known in every frontier.

I can return His love to others dear,
Mainly with folks who need to persevere.
Happy birthday dear Lord of our atmosphere,
Please help us bring peace to Your world's premiere.

—William F. Greene Dec 1989

ST. PETER'S ALTOGETHER

Joe Barnes was just great,
—Didn't hesitate.
Brought ideas new,
—Relieved feelings blue.
It seems that the cure
Was not premature.
'Twas based on things sure
—Makes hearts ever pure.
A lot has to do
With sharing with you,
How one can undo
Destructive thoughts too.
He's taught self esteem,
—We feel we're the creme.
Not better than most,
Too proud just to boast.
Yet sure of ourselves,
—Stand taller than elves,
To communicate
And turnaround fate.
With Christ way inside,
We've nothing to hide.
So when chart'n life's trail,
We're sure not to fail.
You're tops we opine,
Thy lessons do shine.
Thanks be to dear Joe,
We still love you so!

—Bill and Marion Greene 12-1-89

SELF HELP

When I'm feeling uptight and not just right,
I know it'll pass—just the blues in the night.
In times like those I've always seen the light;
Lucky I guess, I don't stay in that plight.
(I empathize with folks who live in fright.)

Once when mine was quite bad I turned to Christ.
My faith, network and will gave me insight
To whip that ogre and to give him flight.
So look within for a li'l grin that might
And you'll raise yourself to a higher height.

—William F. Greene 4 Feb 90

AN INSIDE JOB

When one gets all dressed up for show,
Attention is paid to each detail,
So unmatched colors surely fail
To enable one to bask in glow.

Instead, suppose we'd dress the heart.
Where in heaven would we begin,
Maybe putting something nice therein?
A little love would be a good start.

Let's say the heart then skips a beat,
Eyes light up and you're smiling big.
Now that'll enliven most any shindig
and you are really dressed complete.

—Bill Greene 13Dec 04

A FRIEND INDEED

If you ever need a friend when distressed
And well you might if with a full life you're blessed.
Your many choices require some quest.
We mortals can find a companion for jest.
Lucky ones have one near when there's unrest.

There are times when more is needed by oppressed
For that nagging burden deep in one's breast.
To close the loop: self-family-friends, request
Guidance from God—in all things manifest.

He works between your heart and mind contest,
So you can release anguish, even anger repressed.
You'll emerge in control again coalesced,
Purposeful, confident by His bequest,

To regain or build your esteem compressed.
Quality time spent with your Lord is best,
A partnership with Him leaves you unstressed.
There are times when more is needed when repressed.

—William F. Greene 28April 1990

TRUST AND FAITH

With Christ in one's heart
And ambition to spare,
With hills of endeavor everywhere,
All one needs do is to start!

Trust in Him is so worthwhile
Pursuits of merit race along
While we hum a favored hymn or song.
(That likely won't go out of style).

—William F. Greene 1991

HARVEST DINNER AT CHURCH

As luck would have it, we were last in line.
Those ahead of us had sat down to dine
And seemed content with the cuisine divine.
It won't be long now until I get mine.
My stomach's growling—Oh how I do pine,
While the friends around us all add up to nine.
Over two hundred souls—that's a good sign,
With nary a frown to make it benign.
All that is missing is fruit of the vine
—Next-to-last supper without any wine.

—Billy Cornflake Sept 1990

TIES THAT BIND

What is there in church that I often find,
More than the folks that to me are quite kind.
First and foremost is our Lord's tie to bind,
Us to one another and Him entwined.

Our children learn too and do us remind,
Of the lore of our faith as they're inclined.
From the loving Sunday School that's designed,
To show compassion that's softly lined.

The Missions that we support are consigned,
To teach by example and prayer combined,
That our faith in Him can be well defined,
Finding peace in our life that's streamlined.

—William F. Greene 17 March 1991

A DINNER PRAYER

Dear Lord, as loyal members of your church,
Know that in your ways we are all in search.

We pray for those on Iraq's cold hillsides,
That oppression and illness soon subsides.

While yet in this valley, as we all dine,
Help us remember that our gifts are Thine.

—William F. Greene 4-15-91

PENTACOST

Celebrate Pentecost a birthday way,
With flowers, ferns and balloons where we pray.
Those red'n yellow shapes like flames with tips,
As warm love expressed through caring lips.

It was fifty days after He arose,
Apostles moved to act by faith that grows.
Then thousands were baptized for a mission,
Breaking bonds of fear and superstition.

Many carried Jesus' message of love,
As far as Rome with His power from above.
People listened and responded in kind,
Thus planting our faith deep in man's mind.

—William F. Greene 19May1991

MADONNA'S KIN

Let's "Hail Mary" with a smile on her face,
The gentlest matron of the human race.
By turning to her when we need her grace,
it's easier our unease to displace.

Then her answers to our fervent appeal
Can present themselves to mend our ordeal.
Faith in Mary and her Son will reveal
The strengths in our bonds that are very real.

Remarkable Mary's where we begin,
As in need we search for answers within.
Each one of us is our Madonna's kin,
Can we recall that when patience wears thin?

—William F. Greene 8Aug92 Vandenberg Village

TO JOE MIXSELL:

Here are some rhymes for use in the pew book
If you use more than one you aren't a crook!

SOME WELCOMES TO OUR CHURCH

1.
Please let us know who you are,
'Specially if you're not up to par.
If we can reach you where you live,
it's easier our care to give.
2.
Every time you come to church
And sit upon this cushioned perch,
Take time to write your time and place,
Then we will know what's your home base.
3.
Your name and check marks mean a lot,
For when you leave that's all we've got.
Thanks for joining us in our prayers
To share in words our Lord declares.
4.
Take a minute to fill this in,
Before our worship we begin.
We're glad you came and surely hope
Your life is on a gentle slope.
5.
Whom you are is so good to know
And that this Sunday you did show.
Coming here will help you to glow.
Your sign-up lets us tally ho!

6.
Dear visitors, please take the time.
Your presence with us rings a chime.
Numbers alone don't bring us cheer,
We like to know that you are here!
7.
If on this pad please write your name,
You'll help us play an office game.
We'll know who's here and who is not
—You're more than just an afterthought.
These rhymes that I've thoughtfully wrought
Are the ones that I hope you sought . . . .

—Billy Cornflake 9-6-92

BROADCASTING

Tell it over the hill and everywhere!
How your life has changed and given you flair,
With courage steadfast, how you can dare,
To praise our Lord's name with heart 'cause you care!
If you and your mate are a Christian pair,
Show all by example, His love so fair!

—William F. Greene 16 Aug. 1991

A CHRISTMAS INSTITUTION

Why do reindeer fly in the sky?
—Because we fancy it, that's why!
The one up front has a proud name,
One that has given Santa fame.

Known not to shirk nasty weather,
Brings children and toys together.
Without Rudolph, our Christmas cheer
Would seem a trifle insincere.

He's shown the way for some years now,
His red nose is the cats meow!
If Rudolph has a son I hope,
He has the nose with which to cope!

—Billy Cornflake 12-14-91

CELEBRATING LITTLE JOE'S BIRTH

A red rosebud in our sanctuary,
For the new son of Tom and Kimberlee.
Joseph Thomas LeBlanc surely's the one,
Who by now we hope has learned to have fun.

Uncle Jim from Newberry Park was there
And so was Grandma Fern to show her care.
It is also Mother's day for all moms,
So here in our church, we all read psalms

Little Joe, you're two months and one week old
And were born in early March, it sure was cold.
Go ahead,find happiness on this earth,
We need you to provide some of the mirth.

—William F. Greene 12 May 1991

MY BAPTISM. HOW IT REALLY WAS!

Two pretty blondes at the Baptismal font,
Located near the altar, way up front,
One was Kaitlin Jane, the other her mom.
When passed to Reverend Freund, lost her aplomb.
Jennifer took her back, restoring calm;
Ernie moistened her hair with Baptism balm.

Mrs. Jacobsen, Jenny's Principal,
Gave the Christian Commitment, an earful.
Which means that your church wants you to succeed,
Caring for others is part of our creed.
Katy, we pray for good things in your life
And someday that you'll be a happy wife!

—William F. Greene 12 May 1991

EASTER LOVE TO MY
GRANDCHILDREN AND FRIENDS

An Easter bunny's so cuddly and warm,
He's tame, no wonder in that lovely form.
So spare him the raging of spring-time storm
And keep him inside in his caged dorm.

Does resurrected Jesus like to share
Heavenly triumph with a lowly hare?
Of course he would, isn't it only fair-
That bunny responds as you smooth his hair.

While the Easter bunny's not everywhere,
Loving him is an expression of care.
The teachings of Christ that once were so rare,
Cry out in happiness–a bunny's there!

—Billy Cornflake Easter 1992

ON HIM

Our God is more than man well meant
Though He was made of firmament.
As a lad of twelve he was sage,
Advising men four times his age.

Compassion always was his theme,
Loving people was his grand dream.
The legacy we have from Him,
Is faith with love, His synonym.

—William F. Greene 10-30-92 VV

FAITH WITH LOVE

Unbending faith—unlike true love
Must stand firm and should rise above
Compromise with devilish design,
An absolute in this world of Thine.

True love, more open to all needs,
One's own as well as one's deeds.
Awareness of another's plight
Can comfort and relieve their fright.

Loving self's not selfish to do,
Showing your merit thru and thru.
Philos—one's love for fellow man
—Embodiment of a Christian.

Faith with love then 's on solid ground,
Enabling us all to rebound
From life's dark surprises we know
So we can move on all aglow.

—William F. Greene 10-15-92 VV

A DOUBLE EXCLAMATION !!

Mothers and Others, a tribute to moms,
Is another of our Church's phenoms.
One hundred twenty-nine joined in the fun
And that was only exclamation One!
Today on Mothers Day Ernie declared
For mothers of all time, honor is shared.
From listening to mending and tending needs,
All moms heard. "Thank Yous:"
For their loving deeds.
Great great grandmothers in Church all were Proud,
Those three happy gals stood up in the crowd.
Then all younger moms were praised in return,
The way Ernie used to show our concern.
Soon a Mary and Martha, the first M and Ms,
Contrasted life's values in scorn and gems.
The latter's joy, just like a canary,
Shared in Christ's message, a visionary.
By receiving love, one prepares to give
The finest example of how we live.
Mothers show love in caring and touch.
Returning some then, isn't asking too much!

—William F. Greene 10 May 1992

SPIRITED DINING

Our fellow church-members come out in droves,
Whenever someone turns on the cook stoves!

So church breakfasts given under the spire,
Are out of frying pan, into the choir.

—Billy Cornflake 10-16-92

I'VE GOT MINE

Angels like flappers, kick up their heels,
having fun is what each one of 'em feels.
We each need an angel that'll join in
And provide our lives with a little spin.
An angel at my shoulder does entice
Deep and enduring feelings of paradise,
Urging me on to satisfy my dreams,
While sorting out some that 're only schemes.
Maybe now the devil will leave me be,
For two's company and a crowd is three!

—Billy Cornflake 10-26-92

A PREDICLAMENT — ODDLY ENOUGH

Dan's bankroll, no bottomless pit,
With six daughters he had a fit.
He gave five their weddings fine.
Who'd marry his last fraulein?
Finding her prince and wanting more,
Dan figured he'd end up poor.
so he thought creatively,
"You elope in mystery
And you'll earn a potpourri."

"Hmm" they thought "That'd be neat
And would be a trick complete,
Running off in an old car
To Las Vegas, not too far.
Our friends would snicker 'n laugh
When they read our telegraph.
What a different way to fly,
Matrimony on the sly!"

—Billy Cornflake 11-2-92

HE SAYETH

"Now I lay me down to sleep,
Here among my braying sheep.
Watchful am I for the wolves
And any predator that moves.
I'll guide them to lesser fare
To ensure they get their share.
My sheep tho' are quite special,
Their survival is essential,
For mankind can make or break
This place for heaven's sake."

—William F. Greene 1-16-93

HE'S ALWAYS THERE
(A modern Psalm)

These days it doesn't seem so odd
to renew my faith in God.
When times are lean I seek our Lord,
For by my needs He's never floored.
He helps me see a pathway through
Those miseries that can subdue,
Popping ideas in my brain
That hitherto were not germane.
My Counselor in times of need,
He picks me up so I succeed!

—William F. Greene 1993

TRIBULATION

We'll stick together thru thick'n thin,
At times not knowing how to begin.
I know the feeling, having been there,
Yet fearing less because of prayer.

That lesson over many years,
Yields courage and not anguish or tears,
Simply because of sharing the strain,
Releasing faculties in my brain.

If yours works like mine, then it is best
To release that burden in your breast,
To your closest Friend on this earthen place,
'Til sure enough, you've a happy face!

—William F. Greene 12-8-93

FORGIVEN

When one feels hurt by another,
The relationship can smother.
If brushed aside, healing begins,
Like after one's kicked in the shins.

Oh, it can still hurt for awhile,
But healing pain won't stifle smile.
Time then is a friend, thank goodness.
A hearty pair can reminisce.

Some peoples hurts won't go away,
When anger is aroused to stay.
It really magnifies the pain
And so it seems to be insane.

The one who harbors anger hurts
Himself much more when out he blurts:
"You can head for a real hot place,
For you've fallen out of my grace!"

That's when gentleness counts the most,
Two people healing then can toast:
"Thank you Lord for helping us find
That forgiveness helped cure the blind.

—William F. Greene 4-3-93

A GOOD PLACE TO BE

I join with you in church today,
a place where we both like to pray.
Traditional hymns lead with grace
remove deep furrows from a face,
peacefulness and security,
communing with a mystery.

—William F. Greene 3-20-94

CENSUS BY THE MASTER

Will our Lord count the sheep in his flock,
By day, year or celestial clock?
I'm hoping that some black ones slip in,
That is if I'm ever to grin.

Straight-laced living for some is OK,
But then so are rules, to my dismay.
I would keep wild pranks in check,
I think. (I'd have to, or end up in their clink.)

An infinity of serenity
To me would be an obscenity.
Liven things up and alter the pace,
Even a little roadrunner chase!

It will be interesting to see
Just how accommodating I'll be,
So they won't hold my feet to the fire,
Just 'cause I slipped in under the wire.

—Billy Blacksheepflake 9-27-93 PA

REALLY THANKFUL

In giving thanks, let's give something away,
Like love for fellow man astray.
There, but for blessed grace of God go I.
—That can happen in the blink of an eye!

Pray that we can stay the straight and narrow,
Else one just may earn his fill of harrow.
Give and take, our experience in life
Provides the strength for more demanding strife.

By being able to give on and on,
We are a foundation to build upon,
Ever grateful and humble in our hearts,
We can help lift those who need fresh starts.

—William F. Greene 6Nov93

TO OUR JEWISH FRIENDS,
IN RABIN'S GLOW

A season in time we two share,
Hanukkah and Christmases prayer.
One has origins in the other,
Where we have learned to be a brother.
Gentleness and law which grew in time,
Stimulate people through youth and prime.

Israel's resolve backed by Christians,
A moment of truth among nations
Stands tall while adversaries grate,
Show the world how terrible is hate.
An easy fight 's no fight at all,
But the power of faith's our siren call.

—William F. Greene Dec 1993

IN 1741

The Messiah Handel wrote
Long ago that we emote,
Captivates and raises high
Feelings that will multiply.

Its Hallelujah Chorus
Always sure to delight us,
Reaching deep within our soul
As our Lord it does extol!

—William F. Greene 12-14-93

FORWARD LEAPS

Those bold strokes we see now'n then,
Can stem from action laid down by pen:
Ten Commandments Moses received,
Embraced by his people aggrieved;
The Rosetta stone, wrote 3 ways
The way of life Mideast portrays.
Greek poets gave us tragedy,
Accompanied by comedy;
Hammurabi's code, eye for eye,
Instant justice for a bad guy;

Old and New Testaments sustain
Man choosing not to live in vain;
Magna Carta reined in abuse
By malevolent kings obtuse;
Renaissance scientists did find
An arbitrary religious mind;
"Model Parliament" Edward called
became our Congress, overhauled.
And our Bill of Rights for ages hence,
Freedoms decreed as commonsense.

—William F. Greene 12-15-93 2 A.M.

POSSIBILITIES

I know not that my body will fly high,
But my soul and mind may soar to the sky.
I'll meet St. Peter at the pearly gates,
Zoom straight up to him and not hesitate
To praise him for his service to mankind
And pray that to my faults he will be blind.
If he strokes his chin and then lets me pass,
Soon I will be joining an ultra-class.
Somewhere I'll learn what rules there might be,
That provide some order eternally.
Reunions with loved ones in family
And scores of others I'll be glad to "see"
Will affirm that I've arrived gratefully.
—That journey began in antiquity.

Oh, there is my God, Holy Trinity,
With whom I will spend eternity!
I want to cry, for my faith has been true,
He is real and now I share his milieu.
His hand touches me as I kneel and pray.
For once I can't find anything to say.
My Lord and my God I am at your service,
Now that I've crossed over a wide abyss.

I'm pleased that he said, "Bill, do what you can,
Spread good will and happiness, my good man.
Up here in heaven your spirit is free,
Continue to fulfill your destiny.
Much work needs to be done on earth below
And other planets where growth has been slow.
Help me to nurture their faith and goodness.

As much as I've tried, I must confess,
There are some down there who cause much distress.
Steer them toward love and in all good—success.
I'll be with you always here at your side,
And help you whenever troubles abide.
Take time to enjoy in serenity
And Bill, try a little humility."
So here I am now, free as a honey bee,

Much as on earth, it's still up to me.
I had made my own fun since I was three,
So let's see what will tickle my fancy.
Without bills to pay, I am worry-free,
My mate Marion, just where could she be?
My bit of heaven-on-earth constantly,
She's not here yet—I'll wait expectantly.
I can still whisper softly in her ear,
"I love you and miss my delightful dear",
Gaining comfort knowing she has no fear,
As Christ her Lord will not interfere.
At her own good time she'll join me anon.
I can see her now in pastel chiffon.
For her I've waited, I'll wait once more,
'Cause I know what together there's in store.

Meanwhile as each eternal soul I meet,
I share in their memories so discreet.
Moving on to assess heaven's largesse,
3-D can't describe this scene limitless;

The only gravity's seriousness.
Without effort I float—a trailing tress,
Though sensitive to others and they to me.
Without earth, there's no roots for a tree,
Though birds all around sing so happily.
(If dogs are here, they're in misery!)

Oh, there are 8 souls, playing bridge I guess,
And one is trying to make a finesse!
So earthly tricks abound and are OK,
I wonder about a one-line cliche!
Could there be a pecking-order up here?
Will the saints and angels be cavalier?
Slowing to stop is like being on skis,
Doing it right can make someone sneeze.
Though so far everything has been cheery,
This airy flight can be a bit eerie.
Time passes so smoothly I know I've missed
An afternoon nap on which I'd insist.

Once I loved to rhyme most any ol' time,
With a bit of music—even a chime
And teaming with budding musical souls
Achieve some of my dreamed-of ballad goals.
But those times I know are way in the past
And since no one out here is an outcast,
With lots of time for one's fondest desire,
I'll cut loose and let my soul inspire.
Then too, I can enjoy what others do,
Especially a marvelous breakthrough.
Creative genius abounds I find
And sharing is so open, every soul's kind.
Together we might move the universe,
Toward being a better place and not worse.
To transcend fear and even pestilence,
So people can live with great confidence.

If sometime it would get crowded up here,
With life becoming in each biosphere,
A planetary heaven on each earth,
They'd like that, so let's give it all we're worth!

With no clock or calendar anywhere
Type "A" behavior has been changed with care,
But it could take awhile if it's pronounced.
(Miracles though, often come unannounced!)
So far I haven't seen any TV.
Most souls find joy conversationally.
There's lots of listening when one speaks up,
It's a way each has to fill up one's cup.

There's no welfare or any needy soul,
Or any infirm for one to cajole.
Disabled are cured as they enter here.
Spirits it seems are loaded with good cheer.
Race too, seemed to vanish passing those gates.
Hatreds and envy St. Peter cremates.
Quite pleased to still find some macho in me,
That assures a mite of identity.
I've still many an unanswered question,
Really too many for me to mention,
But where are my mom, dad and dear brother Joe
And earlier ancestors I don't know.
Missing persons are every where I'm told.
Finding them is a joyful nugget of gold!

I may never end this search in future,
But it certainly is my great adventure!
Imagine how wonderful it would be
When these impressions are reality!

—William F. Greene 3-19-94

As we begin this Easter Week
let's all be just a little meek . . .

REMEMBRANCE

Eastre, ancient goddess of Spring,
Gave up her name to Christ the King.
For it was in Spring He arose,
After His Good Friday pathos.

Few recall that goddess today,
But to the King, they'll kneel and pray.
Giving all for His followers,
They carry on as believers.

—William F. Greene 3-25-94

UNSLEEPY

When sleepless, there's a dividend,
The time alone will be a friend.
Bypassing frowns in that malaise,
Enrich in memories bouquets!

One's mind's a happy birthright,
Turning dismay to delight,
Counting His blessings yet to come,
One sure way to banish glum!

—Billy Cornflake 8-19-94

ARE WE OK?

At times when things 'tween us went wrong
And life became deserted song
We'd long to find that middle ground
Where both our comfort zones are found.

Then one would ask "Are we OK?"
The answer sad though showed the way
For us to mend those feelings strained
With empathy that was right brained.

Quicker then than had we stayed sour,
We brightened-up like a spring flower,
Restored by faith in openness
With lots of help by His largesse.

—Billy Cornflake 20Nov94

LOVE HONOR AND OBEY

We can love honor and obey
If we haven't along the way.
Understanding what it all means,
Can help us be great kings and queens.
On anniversaries fulfill,
While warming one's mate from a chill.

Considering three kinds of love,
Each of which are gifts from above,
There is fulfillment in each one,
Praised by Father, Spirit and Son.
Making room in our lives for them
We wear a royal diadem:

Philos or love of fellow man-
Compassion, courtesy's the plan.
Mother Theresa's caring life,
Is a model relieving strife.
One's thoughtfulness in word and deed,
Are all part of this loving breed.

Agape love is God's own style,
In which He goes the extra mile,
To comfort those of us in need,
Whether or not we follow His creed.
Embracing and dependable
Its power is incredible.

Eros reigns from our teen years on
Under often hidden neon.
A compelling force in our lives,
Always welcome when it arrives.
Though some see just a seamy side,
We mostly take that all in stride.

Honoring one's mate is fine art,
And heart-to-heart's a way to start.
Respect and patience with one's spouse,
Will make for peace around the house.
Anger is known to have no place,
If each would wear a happy face.

Who is the boss here anyway?
For some guys that's the only way.
It only works because of fear,
Damping a marital career!
There's a leader for each domain,
With teamwork on each others brain.

Love, honor and obey you say?
When mutual, it's no cliche.
Those words are spoken to instill
Charity in one's loving skill.
As hearts and minds do intertwine
The best of two will then combine.

—William F. Greene 20Dec1994

INNER CALM

Sunday morning in church with kin,
we're searching for our souls within,
to serve the Master in His way,
hence forward on every day.

Our woes seem small compared to those,
hungry, in terror and in no clothes.
We pray that we can give much more
of time and wealth, evening score.

Feeling good is a basic need,
which one can do within his creed.
Bless us all in our daily lives,
as each one of us truly strives.

—William F. Greene 6-26-94 LPC

When times are tough we may implore
Help me to mend my every flaw . . .

FAITH REVEALED

Gray hair in church is about half,
Worn by some who walk with a staff,
Belies commitment to their Lord,
Even as life's travails have gored.

Undying faith in Him above,
Much like unconditional love
Sustains mortals body and soul
Striving for that eternal goal.

Amazing grace is here to stay
Sustaining us every day,
With bright rays it does emit,
A share saved for every spirit.

—William F. Greene 2-5-95

HORSEFEATHERS!

Decent behavior deserves much more
Than scorn from others by the score,
However often it seems to me
It is all about controlling thee.

Take heart those who are vilified,
Remember Him and how he died.
The philistines still abound these days,
So simply ignore them in their craze.

Counterattack if you really must
—A proper parry and a firm thrust,
Then they will learn for to play the game
That after battle they might be lame.

—Billy Cornflake April 1994

54

ONE WAS CHOSEN

The Pharaoh's daughters, were so fond
Of a baby found in a pond.
That was three thousand years ago,
A tale since childhood we all know.

When all grown-up Moses would learn
To respond to his God's concern,
There were times he'd feel unprepared,
But measured up for those he cared.

While parting oceans may not be,
The kind of task for you or me,
A little boy with just his thumb
Saved a dike 'til others could come.

—Billy Cornflake 2-5-95

DEALER CHOICE

Praying for an outcome fine,
To our Lord who is divine,
Why not leave it in His hands,
For then 'tis His will commands.

Who knows best just what to do,
To make an event come true,
Mortal beings, you and I
Or our Leader in the sky?

—William F. Greene 11-19-95

THREE LOVES

Of all kinds of love, each one I will toast.
Has one of 'em risen to be the most?
Anyone can determine which it is,
Or if each be a third of loving bliss.
Agape, Philos and Eros make three.
Which you may find in your family tree.

Agape, an all embracing god love,
Was created by our Master above.
Given to us unconditionally,
Which we can do as 'round Christmas holly.
Detached tho' it harbors no hate,
One of the reasons a giver feels great.

Philos is also taken from the Greek,
In practice, really it holds no mystique.
Brotherly love can be easy to give,
Provided there's Agape where we live!
It works, believe me, time tested and true,
Coming home to roost with your follow through.

Now Eros is the most selfish of all,
Enjoyers of it are having a ball.
Thriving on passions it often inflames
The hearts of all lovers, both males and dames.
Eros is part of the family plan
That long ago Adam and Eve began.

—William F. Greene 10-2-94

A SIGN

Success stories with people scorned
In relationships I have mourned,
In truth were enriched by a prayer
After I had been in despair.

A lesson learned is pray much more
For relationships to restore
As soon as they appear to be
Short-changed of Christianity.

—William F. Greene 7-3-94

A GOOD PLACE TO BE

I join with you in church today,
A place where we both come to pray.
Traditional hymns led with grace
Remove deep furrows from a face,
Peacefulness and security,
Communing with His mystery.

—William F. Greene 3-20-94

NOW AND THEN

Who among us can say in truth
That we have loved our Lord since youth
And still believe his promises,
While deploring his nemesis.

Who still can relate fervently
To future thought as heavenly.
The nature of that place on high
And what will be there in the sky.

Those afterlife conceptions found
In Egypt where in underground
Remains and other artifacts
Seem joined with their idols compacts.

Missing is the forgiveness we
Have known in Christianity,
With love and hope and faithfulness
An ultimate living success.

—William F. Greene 1995

58

PREJUDGE

In the churchyard under the cross,
it reminds me just who is boss,
so whenever I crowd the line
I remember Him at that shrine.

—William F. Greene 4-19-95

SUCCEEDING

I love people who strive and strive,
The stuff that keeps them all alive.
When self indulgence overcomes
And one's life then no longer hums,
Some secret power down deep within
May overcome and help to win.
So family, God and striving will
Make over and their cup to fill.
Striving too in life's tragedies
With that same guidance, return ease.
The Greene family knows in spades
That perseverance makes no trades,
Ever onward with heads held high,
Believe in self, God and then try!

—Billy Cornflake 10-1-96

ON THANKSGIVING

We give thanks for the gift of life
And promise of an afterlife.
For striving we give thanks to him
Keeping us focused, shy of whim.
Rewards of purposeful living
Help us to be more forgiving
Success in what we do so well
Is why in prayer we choose to dwell
As the wide world learns of this power,
Teamwork with one's Lord will flower,
Budding and blooming brilliantly,
So winning is no mystery.

—William F. Greene 6Nov96

THANK YOU

When thanking Him remember *those,*
who helped to keep us on our toes.
A friend, a mentor or one's spouse,
who caution us if we would grouse
and use that energy to grow,
producing something apropos.

Friendship itself deserves to be
honored truly in high degree.
As life unfolds and years slip by
a friend's value one can't deny,
so gratitude in voice or *prose*
is reassuring when he knows.

—William F. Greene 6Nov96

Y-2 EASTER

When the Easter Bonnet was a craze
Men wore top hats so ladies would gaze.
Over time that ego trip would fade,
As alas did Easter Parade.
Did the Easter bunny then bounce in,
With some wearing a chocolate grin
And the egg roll on the lawn,
After some while until we would yawn.
Oh sure, we still make Easter funday
After Sunrise Service we play
And celebrate a resurrection,
That followed our Lord's crucifixion.
Easter's survived millenias two.
It's because of the believers who,
Humbly abide by those teachings He,
By example taught us patiently.

—William F. Greene 3-16-99

PLIMOTH PLANTATION, 1621

In humility, Pilgrims prayed.
The gratitude that they displayed
Went far beyond a thank-you note,
Remembered still in grand parade.

A Norman Rockwell down-home scene,
Lingers softly in mind serene.
His generations so eager,
As gramps carves the turkey cuisine,

This American melting pot
Welcomes all, dark brown to Scot,
Who look to us for calm reprieve,
Oft to escape from a despot.

Every soul who finds our shores
And lends his shoulder to some chores,
Erases quickly, memories sad,
As soon this country he adores.

From rocky coast to beach of sand,
Newcomers hustle, proudly stand,
While they too bow in reverence,
For they have found this Promised Land.

—William F. Greene 1999

MMM BEGINS!

Anno Domini Two Thousand,
The Third Christian Millennia,
Can clearly sense from Galilee
What this, our world, is meant to be.

Mankind's progress, a wonderland,
Honored with Ave Maria,
Ever mindful of Mothers plea,
Compassion to help us be free.

Her Son for us, took a stand grand,
"Love thy neighbor" panacea,
As in golden rule's decree
Often 'tis said, can we agree?

—William F. Greene 30 Dec. 1999

A LAW & ORDER THANKSGIVING

This new millennium Thanksgiving Day
May give us pause to reflect as we may.
In earliest recorded history,
Societies oft used brutality,
Were unforgiving, an, eye for an eye
And ignored Socratic philosophy.

—William F. Greene Nov 16-2000

SUDDENLY IN 1620 A.D.

The Mayflower Compact, Pilgrim's destiny,
Established their New World rules and restraint
That worked for them but today seem so quaint.
The essence though was preordained order
As honorable gentlemen would concur.
The Colonies struggled with many schemes
Resolved by Constitutional themes.
We fashion still and interpret each law,
For some at times may stick in one's craw.
We are thankful for what laws have been made,
Are applied to all and hence no charade.

—William F. Greene Nov 2000

RECOLLECTIONS

America grows on ideas
And hard work,
Continuing traditions
As technology soars.

Age old skills like building roads
Use giant machines toting loads,
Reducing workmen's heavy toil.
At home, at work and in-between,

Info of course,
With privacy control
To express our fancies
Where ever we please.

We celebrate this Labor Day,
Mostly in an old-fashioned way.
A barbeque, an outing in a park,
Or concert before or after dark.

That three-day weekend guaranteed,
Except for store workers—in need . . .

—William F. Greene Sept 2000

THE MAN-GOD

Two millennia of Easter's rise
And still we pray in wonderment.
His resurrection beyond our skies,
An afterlife so provident,
That man for ages has prepared
To join his Lord, a Trinity,
Because in part, we know He cared,
With faith, hope, love and charity.

—William F. Greene 4-16-00

KIDDIES KNOW

The little children He loved so,
All blessed by His heavenly glow,
Respond in kind and thoughtful ways
Through the ages to modern days.

—William F. Greene 4-16-00

FOR EASTER IN 2001

As Easter lilies bloom and grow,
They symbolize in purest white,
A resurrection in the night
And Christians sense an afterglow.

His message, Love with faith in Him,
Repeats around our globe each year.
Even as despots rule with fear,
Their suppressed masses hope won't dim.

With truth, one's doubts demystify.
The promise then is we will rise
And eternal life is the prize,
By faith alone when judgment's nigh.

—William F. Greene 27Mar2001

POST EQUINOX

As flowers bloom in May-
A wet April had its say!
A verdant valley of flower fame,
Grows anew in the wild or tame,

Celebrated by Choir's chords,

For Him on high, our Lord of Lords.

—William F. Greene Mar. 2001

SOME OTHER WAYS

In thought about a change in state,
Say in relation to one's mate,
When misfortune of any kind
Strikes home altering state of mind,
With implications so severe
One grows inward, perhaps in fear.
How then can one remain the same,
When that misfortune is to blame?
As surely as it strains one's soul,
Former feelings then take a toll,
Leaving only a shallow shell,
Where before love would cozy dwell.
Such limitations need not stall,
A depth of love that did enthrall,
With feelings spent—an alternate,
May be found to improve one's fate,
When acts of kindness show one's care
And they shine through like fervent prayer.

—William F. Greene Nov 2001

AN EASTER PRAYER WHILE AT WAR

Enable our hearts and mind in prayer,
Through a rather brief Lenten span,
With strengthening faith in God and man,
For His resurrection we hope to share.

While striving to emulate His ways,
Honoring our Savior's sacrifice,
We stand in awe of his heavenly rise,
Each of us offering our faith bouquets.

—William F. Greene 2003

A SPECIAL KIND OF FRIEND

When times are tough, Christ is my rainbeau,
The beau known to be master of care,
As uncertainty looms, I seek him there,
And through him, I am able to grow.

Waiting, waiting for me to call,
Patient and willing to share with me,
Wherever I am, my life trustee,
Dependably in any rainfall.

His access line is never busy,
A toll-free call, no cell phone at all.
Silently as in gentle snowfall,
Or spoken on high or a valley.

This partnership from dawn 'til I sleep,
Carries me through even frightful days,
As He helps turn them into bouquets,
Whether I'm joyful or tend to weep.

Thank you, Jesus!

—Bill Greene 10-12-03

AYUDARME (HELP ME)

Lord, do I honor you in all I do?
Help me, whenever I stray,
When your values I don't display,
As thought, speech and acts miscue.

Much as in Your life here on earth,
I face challenges to my faith,
At times accepting someone's scathe,
Which can lower my own self worth.

Daily, I share your company,
On arising and through the day,
Knowing you listen to what I say
And refresh with your gifts so many.

Still, to resist, I'm helpless alone
—Those spontaneous threats to my soul
Need your strong shield to keep me whole,
Whole in You, to ensure I've grown.

Earnestly,
—William F. Greene 9-23-04

ON LOVE CREATIONS

Jesus precious gift, our salvations,
Released through saved hearts new creations,
Where oft' objective means before,
Was how folks tried to do much more.
Since then, His love would dominate
And enlarge what we could create,
As one's heart then comes into play,
Especially when we'd pause to pray.
How beneficial is His gift!
In all we do, it adds uplift,
As ever mindful we can say—
"Thank You Lord, for our heart's bouquet"!

—Bill Greene 15Feb 2005

ON FAITH IN CHRIST

His body slain, His body lain,
In a garment, that would remain,
When a large stone closing that tomb,
Was moved to find an empty room.

Time would pass then He'd reappear,
Recounted as five hundred near.
His resurrection noted well,
A most endearing story to tell.

While this short tale can never be
Full solution of the mystery,
Faith, dear ones, for Thomases all,
Shall be the case for doubt overcall.

On Reflection
—William F. Greene 2-25-04

ON MEMORIES

God given, to humans delight,
Good ones, of course our hearts do warm,
Creating smiles and endless charm,
To which we hold with all our might.

Bad ones though, may wither away,
Thanks to His gentle forgiveness
And with his grace He can us bless,
Leaving us with our life's essay.

Avoiding some that scar and hurt,
We can enhance the beauty in,
So memories out yield no chagrin,
Only melodies in one's own concert.

Seldom have we thought that He,
Embraces all of our memories fair,
Yet all the while, He's always there,
And that my friends is no mystery.

A fond memory this . . .
—Bill Greene, 20 June 2004

ON LEADERSHIP

When summer yields to yellow leaves
And our youngsters return to school,
As purposeful learning one believes
Includes faith of our fathers dual.

"Two, you say, there's but one!"
The 2nd say I, "is faith in man".
Jesus, truly God and man-son,
Taught us how to be better than.

His life on earth embraced all men;
Faith in competent leaders skills,
For stout-hearted men win again
And they are gifted with free wills.

Together, we hope with God in prayers
That worthy mankind choose to lead,
Such benevolent portrayers,
Of Christian ideals well inbred.

—Bill Greene 8-10-04

OUR MOTHERS

One day our Mothers are a shrine,
You honor yours as I do mine.
In deference, shall we cite those ways
That Mothers brighten all our days . . .

To Church and Sunday School we went,
Our mothers all were heaven sent.
Honor, fairness with gentleness,
Responsibility—oh yes!

She taught us how to persevere,
And with compassion when sincere,
In family settings we'd recall,
With our offspring that now enthrall.

So as we phone or visit her
And play the family raconteur,
The bonding memories remain,
Embracing all our kin's domain.

We love you, Mom!

—Bill Greene 12April 06

CONNECT THE DOTS

The evidence, goal and route thereto:
He lived was crucified and arose.
That life was one the Father chose,
Eternal life, His promise so true.

Believers we who gather and pray,
Revere His presence in our lives,
As our growing love for Him thrives
And that faith sustains us every day.

Dots and all (Prayer) sharpen our aim,
Like signposts found along the way,
With kindness in the words we say,
A form of love since Jesus came . . .

—Bill Greene 7-17-06

SMILE'S JOURNEY

Unhappiness needs a wholesome smile,
Relieving stresses all of the while.
Notice how others smile contagion,
Softens mood and frown creation!

Isn't that a nice way to start,
Setting the horse before the cart?
While one's smile will open a door,
'Tis warming to follow with more . . .

Committed service of skills with grace,
Add from *WITHIN* to one's glowing face.
While smile alone won't fix a care,
Let's try a shot from the heart in prayer.

—Bill Greene Apr Newsletter 05

AMAZING GRACE "DAD" (C. 1750)

Teen seaman John Newton who sailed
On his fathers ship, wrote this gem
In classic style 'twas his poem,
To save a wretch who'd awfully failed.

As Cap'n, his ship in stormy sea,
Endured that month; his faith would grow,
From a life that'd been mighty low,
To an England Church Pastor, he.

His hymns and sermons synergy,
Enabled him to London inspire,
As his legend spread like wildfire,
Unveiling much of God's ministry.

'Tis known Dad John Newton had learned,
As us other dads ever since,
Those hard lessons that made us wince,
Provide strength in Him we have earned.

—Bill Greene, June 2005

WARMTH OF LOVE

When in love at top of your game,
Life's a breeze, like flying trapeze,
Making other emotions seem tame.

When one's partner returns the same
And you know it's more than to please,
Praise the Lord, two hearts are aflame!

—William F. Greene 12June 2005

HEARTBEAT TIME

Affirm endearment every year,
Even daily if you prefer,
(Which I'll bet will surely please her)
When she's the one you long to hold dear.

If she's not yours yet, say a prayer.
A heavenly assist will do
Enough, to turn her heart toward you,
As she learns how much you care.

Since Love's Jesus favorite theme,
Count on Him to be a real pro,
To have and be loved, simpatico,
Knowing you're on the first team!

—William F. Greene 2005

OOPS

Watch out below when attitudes slip.
It helps to note soon that stagnation,
For needed is determination,
As "Omigosh, I'm losing my grip"!

Fix it before someone sees it first.
Go it alone if that's your style,
Yet may I suggest something worthwhile?
Our best Friend's there to avoid the worst

For those bi-polar, they'll need more . . .
Though many of us recover quick,
Like within the hour is no trick.
A simple prayer say, "Help me restore".

Seizing such moments changes course,
Distraction maybe, but mood's resolved,
By upbeat charm so cares are solved,
With inner peace and no remorse.

—Bill Greene July 2005

YES

When someone we know recovers well
There's a glorious story to tell!
By answering all our hopes and prayers
We've learned among His believers,
Felicity as promised to us,
Is oft' rewarded with a plus!

Then, "Thank You Lord" meditation,
Deepens rapport through one-on-One.
So, heaven closeness, as we strive
In fulfillment while we're alive,
Is there for us to acquire,
On His celestial amplifier.

—Bill Greene 15June 2005

HIGH 5S FOR JESUS

(INTERACTIVE CHRISTIANITY)

Shall we give High 5s for Jesus?
Christian relations stronger than whim,
Our showing of accepting Him
While His open gift embraces us.

On His policy, we're insured,
And can confidently meet each test,
Expecting to do our very best
With His lasting love assured.

—Bill Greene 12Aug 05

You may offer me and others these "High 5 s" . . .

82

A CHRISTIAN PARTY
(Joins Church and Mate)

To elect our God, Let us vote!
His adversary is quite well known,
Intruding often in tempting tone,
Even converting some, sad to note.

Lovingly, embrace our God on high,
Going where He leads us, without fear,
As those fears vanish when He is near,
For our lives with Him, amplify.

—Bill Greene 12Aug 05

Are we "registered"?

CLOSING A LOOP

The wisp—a thought—though reverent
Can flash away in a moment.
Can all the king's horses and men
Combine to retrieve it again?

Let not that be as we pause in prayer,
In firm connectedness to share.
Sensitive to how He tugs your heart
And grand feelings that does impart.

Propelled or moved to act in kind,
As that feeling imbeds in your mind,
Your needs are charted to act upon,
Soon—before it has come and gone!

—Bill Greene 22Oct 05

ON LOVING JESUS

We adore Jesus
Out of earned respect.
(Yeah, the multitudes cured)
First as a babe,
Then a twelve year old
Temple teacher
And of course,
His disciples leader,
With Love!

Then, crucified,
Resurrected and yes, elevated!
—So in our hearts,
Minds, souls and faith,
We commit to Him,
Above all else,
With our whole being.

It's thrilling
To write to Him,
About Him—and
Especially, His Love.

As did He,
Would we give up
Our lives for Him?
—We certainly have
For country, Family,
Even strangers.
Though likely,
We won't have to,

Gratefully now,
He smoothed our path
To eternal life
With Him,
As His servant and friend.,
Evermore.

—Prayerfully by Bill Greene 21Nov 2005

CHRISTMAS STORY RENEWAL

In touching hearts, the Christmas story,
Well told by Luke, still lives today
And like Wise Men, we honor and pray,
Offering love for the Christ child's glory!

So we spread the little Babe's joy,
And our love spills over the brim,
In activities declared for Him,
Including—yet more than a child's toy.

The Christmas spirit brings out our best,
Warm feelings and gifting, boundless ways,
As Church folk happily sing His praise,
Knowing in Him we are truly blessed!
Happy birthday, Jesus!

—Bill Greene 21Nov. 2005

A QUIET CONVERSATION

Can we resolve to talk with Him,
Say, offering an inner thought,
For His guidance, earnestly sought,
While humming a favorite Hymn?

Gentle feelings as we converse
Flavor relationships each day
From what He relates as we pray
With followers in His universe.

—Softly, Bill Greene Dec. 05

THOUGHTFUL VALENTINES

A valentine is nice to get
And special for it shows your hand,
While making it your best one yet,
More than hearts drawn in the sand.

Quite like commitment to our Lord,
It's meant forever and deeply too,
Not wishy-washy on your word,
But contemplative through and through.

—Bill Greene '06

Lovers woo and ballyhoo,
and hopefully it's really true . . . .

ON LENT

Each Lenten fast is meant to be
A cleansing of the mind to find
One's faith again in Him refined,
Yet through the heart to reverie.

Wholesome, open relationships
Can build one's friends eternally.
Soon if not eventually,
Replacing negative's eclipse.

As mentally we venture in
Christ's kingdom where He keeps a place,
For each of us to Him embrace,
A prize we each pray that we'll win.

—Bill Greene 31Jan 2006

EASTER PARADE

As Easter Parade's arrogant show,
Had moved its vanity way off scale,
Such excesses were bound to fail,
In Easter messages brilliant glow.

Christ's torture, death and resurrection,
Crystallized our faith, hope and love,
Which, with other gods was unheard of,
So now we share in His affection.

This gorgeous Spring as our faith renews
Let us recall His good news!
Jesus Christ came here for us to save,
Now we too can escape from the grave.

Meanwhile,
As we grow through practiced Lent
We've stronger purpose in fulfillment.
Keeping Him in mind in each endeavor,
While planning to be with Him forever.

—Bill Greene 19March 2006

CONGENIAL DAD

That shoulder or a forearm poke,
How we greet Dad, a virile joke.
We're glad that he gets on so well,
Those years upbringing us compel.

Our special connections stay firm,
As age-old memories confirm.
They met the test of time secure
As our reunions reassure.

He's still ahead in our golf game,
Because my aim is not as tame,
Yet never rubs it in to hurt
Or shadow advice to me assert.

I praise the Lord for what He's done
My Dad is surely a home run.
Mutual respect is so alive,
It keeps our love in overdrive.

Thanks, Dad,

—Bill Greene 2006

GOOD OL' SUMMERTIME

One day for Mom, another for Dad,
The kiddies tho', claim all summer,
For without it, what a bummer,
'Twould make all of our youth so sad.

Beach time helps to soothe their souls,
Or mountain hikes to fireside song,
In troop or group, where they belong,
Nature close, as God's presence extols.

Vacation Bible School's for those,
Who want and need His enrichment,
Along with fun that's heaven sent,
All with fine leaders that we chose.

Then there's the treasures children find,
Creatively striving to achieve
With lots of home-spun make-believe,
Immersed in family love so kind.

—Bill Greene, Summer 2006

JESUS WOULD SAY:

Put your hand in mine
And
Let your whole world shine
while
Softening heart and mind
To be
More gentle and kind.
for
In my house, love sustains
So
The new you ordains.
In
Loving you proclaim
Among
All our heavenly friends
Then,
My Father and Holy Spirit Rejoice.

—William F. Greene July 2006

ON LOVE

Marital love with its many hues,
Has clues that can enlighten ones views.
For me it came dressed in His grace,
As in time it found the heart place.
If trust was not there to be found,
Our love wouldn't have left the ground.
Though lost, through Him, I could again, see,
—Knowing true love had been mystery.

After many years, love's strong headlight
Calms me because of Jesus foresight.
Whether or not in the driver's seat,
Love's presence makes life more complete.
I delight the comfort in being near,
Likely in reverence to my Dear.
Fulfillment on grand scale is mine,
—It's been polished to enduring shine.

Erotics have their role, for sure,
Beginning with some smiles demure.
Yet, surpassed by relationships,
Sealed in mind and soul by loving lips.
Never alone in any scene
With love, my pathway is serene.
So when troubles mount and love is there,
Relax in faith, with love in prayer.

—Bill Greene 9-12-06

Though my preacher said "You're in love with love",
—Even that though, must come from above.

HOW GREAT THOU ART
ON VETERAN'S DAY

We like to sing that fine old hymn,
While stirring us, it pleases Him.
Gratitude we hold for our Lord
Was earned by His blood that poured.

Patriots have died for us too,
Protecting the red, white and blue.
Many are they who would not yield,
Honored still in church and afield.

How great they were and many still
Covered with rose and daffodil.
While those alive will shed a tear,
Memories saving us from fear.

In honoring them, we honor Him,
With heavenly host of Seraphim.
For in Him we trust timelessly,
Each of us, a Christian Trustee.

—Bill Greene 10-21-06

I'LL BE SEEING YOU . . .

As music reminds us of hopeful times,
So religious experience
Restores that hope.
—It could well be
The music of Christ in our lives
That moves us to accomplish
Those best choices, with his guidance.

Drumbeats of time
Hasten us along the way,
To be sure that we achieve our goal.
A goal for self, family
Or community.
So, with Him in our network of choice,
All things conceived can be come real.

—Bill Greene 10-24-06

HUMBLE BE

While Christmas for children charms,
Our effort though can bring some glow,
To those who live away from home.

As we walk down their lonely halls,
The distant look their faces show,
Unsettles as they seek your glance.

No visitor has come to share,
Or family to offer care,
Yet attendants there are aware.

Whatever mind is left to know,
Is dwarfed by hearts their smile creates.
—Of all the care they need the most,

Are your interest and kindly words.
—Though few, they sow a seed,
A loving memory of the moment . . .

—Bill Greene 11-17-06

A BIRTH GLORIOUS

To fathom His resurrection,
There had to be His wondrous birth,
A manger scene that Kings would share.
Still celebrated 'round world's girth.

A babe delights, either boy or girl,
Our Jesus though redeemed each soul,
Much more precious than any pearl,
For His coming has made us whole.

He offers us Faith, Hope and Love,
To cherish and transfer about,
With Love that He well interwove,
Firmly planted, without a doubt.

Jesus, welcome to our homes and hearts,
No chimney need Ye slither down,
We've learned Your love to us imparts,
That wholeness of which you are renown.

Thanks for coming, Lord,
Please stay as long as You can.

—Bill Greene 17Nov 2006

ON A LONELY WALK

Having lost both legs in an Iraq town,
'Twas there an I.E.D. was blown.
When Rescue came, I was clear "out".
With naught below knees, I'd cry and shout.

We were all sent there to make men free
And most of us went happily.
Now I lean hard on thee, Lord,
Yet vividly re-live how I was gored.

Still please Lord, enable me to cope,
I'll muster some courage and hope.
Tho' others died there in their prime,
A thought occurs to me this time:

You know I must be duty-bound,
To help survivors hurt profound,
Face the ordeal while trusting You,
To start and get a life anew

Way down deep there within my soul,
Helping wounded troops is my goal.
Let's put in place a plan together,
Then nurture me like my big Brother.

To apply myself I promise-
The long hours to get it right.

—by Bill Greene 11-25-06 age 80, Ret. US Navy

ON BELIEVING

Empowered by Christ's birth and life,
We honor Him in many ways,
Undaunted by our worldly strife,
To emulate him all our days.

Luke transcribed for us to read,
Jesus simple and humble birth,
Soon to be known with Magi's lead,
Our savior's incredible worth.

Some written in century one,
Encouraged men to believe in Him,
Becoming testament to the Son.
—Now believers aren't out on a limb.

—Bill Greene 12-20-06

LISTENING WELL

Especially when we are all alone,
And no one calls on our small cell phone,
Such a quiet time in prayer
Meets our need for that certain care.

An opportunity to say,
Just what tweaks your mind that day.
Then patience in a listening mode
Does help in breaking the Lord's code.

He'll steer your thoughts to action plans
And they will not be *also ran's.*
His work's not finished till you start,
To make things happen from your heart.

Where motivation, backed by brains,
So often leads to prayed for gains,
For which we humbly bow one's head,
Or simply read the bible instead.

—Bill Greene 12-20-06

TRYSTING IN OUR SECRET PLACE

While reaching out for Jesus hand,
He stirs our hearts with feelings grand.
A partner not so silent He,
Still living there in mystery.

We're lifted up from cares and woe,
So that we can thrive in His glow,
Using His advice in judgments made,
To live our lives in no charade.

He's been there all along we know,
Gently nudging us so we grow.
He will help us to mend our ways,
As long as in our hearts He stays.

His Agape love for us all,
Permits each one to overhaul,
The ways we selflessly proclaim,
With Valentines that can enflame.

Jesus our welcome honored guest,
The Holy Grail of our long quest,
Remain with us and our world in prayer,
Promoting love and kindness there.

Light hearted lovers, appear on scene,
Wholesome, endearing and serene,
All the while, they share in His view,
To help each other, that they'll do.

—Bill Greene 12Jan 2007

A VALENTINE TO BE

Come on along and venture in
A life-style that will warm your heart.
Togetherness that should impart
Excitement that just won't wear thin.

With His blessing as we share lives.
Learning each others many ways,
While blending them in fresh arrays,
Praying that true love arrives.

—Bill Greene 2008

VALENTINES AT WORK

Light hearted lovers, appear on scene
Wholesome, endearing and serene,
All the while, they share in His view,
With their Valentines warm break through.
They're hoping the other will know,
How their tender thoughts will grow,
Into a bonding they hope to make,
As Christian's wed, f'heaven's sake.
They'll tread together in all kinds of weather.

—Bill Greene 2008

Easter celebrates by way of the moon,
Though we celebrate the Man-God who rose.

EASTER 2008

When Christ arose, new life began.
Then His brother James carried on that truth,
Strengthened by his faith and relative youth
In ministry during James brief lifespan.

Christ's disciples gave their lives in His name,
As Rome feared that *New Christianity.*
Though He'd coexist in humility,
'Til Rome approved Christians—canceling blame.

Groups today still, the risen Christ deny;
His name in public is quite seldom heard.
For this Christian nation, that is absurd,
Founded in Christ, we should still sanctify.

His love contains ours in everyplace,
In ways we should treat one-another grand,
Meeting all needs, like He fed 5000,
Saving our souls through our faith and His grace.

—Bill Greene 12March 2008

ON REWARDING MOTHERS

In May we celebrate Motherhood,
Which by God's plan promotes our kind
And we're grateful that He's so inclined,
While He makes sure that it is good.

Mothers nurture tots thru teens,
With nary a slip from cup to lip,
Tho' after age ten, it's quite a trip,
Saving their lives and souls it seems.

As the heart of home life she shines,
With gentle manner as in love songs,
She's always there to soothe our wrongs,
Leading us along His life road signs.

"Without Mothers, we aren't much"
As Mark Twain said eloquently,
To remind of that truth eternally,
To practice her love and gentle touch.
Amen.

—Bill Greene 16 April 2008

DEAR DAD

Jokes aside, Dad—I do love you.
Times we've shared live in memory,
Like the time you taught me to ski,
Patient, caring and steadfast true.

Then nudging me to know our Lord,
Helps me still to confide in Him,
In good times and when life is grim,
'Til equanimity's restored.

High Five's that I make with you Dad,
Celebrating the joys we share,
Have made us a special pair,
So for those blessings Dad, I'm glad!
Love, your son, Bill

—William F. Greene 11May 2008

ENTHEOS

A Greek word, root of *enthusiasm,*
It translates into **God in us.**
—Still wonder from where enthusiasm stems?

Our guiding light, and our beacon.
Thank Him for our so many gifts
And wondrous blessings in our lives.

Did we ask for His help ? Maybe.
Did He wait for us to ask ? No.
He's there all the time, on duty.

Enthusiasm, oft spontaneous,
Is because He made us that way.
Or it can grow as we immerse
In creative thought or deed.

Could it grow out of one's envy?
Certainly, borrowed with gratitude
And when pursued with diligence.

Oh, he knows disappointment in us,
When we cross the line into sin
Or sin-like thoughts or perhaps more.

Still with the upper hand, He forgives,
His guarantee for one's strong faith.
There, enthusiastically, **God in us.**

—Bill Greene 17Aug 2008

ON CHRISTIAN TEARS

When we see those tears flow from loving eyes,
Surely they come to us as no surprise,
From singing olden hymns like He Arose,
Christ Jesus he arose . . .

These hints of the flower in His grace,
We sense each day in our worshiping place,
Shamelessly streak down and warming a cheek,
Ever proudly of one's Christian mystique.

Strong emotion then does draw us to Him,
While reason affirms, filling to the brim.
As happiness grows deep within one's breast,
Strengthened by a faith that we have professed.

—Bill Greene, 9/11/2008

ON PLEASING OTHERS

At every level, while alive,
To please other folks, we will strive.
Should that group include our dear Lord,
There is for us a huge reward.

Why yes, we can smile for Jesus,
As we do for folks that please us.
We even do nice things for friends,
Yet, when for Him, sweet dividends.

All the while, our faith comes to mind,
Like in those who share our daily grind.
But our faith in Him means much more,
As Heaven becomes our open door.

—Bill Greene 5Oct 2008

SAVINGS GUARANTEED

Unlimited savings for your souls,
Taxpayer's paradise fully assured,
One's rent and mortgage, they're insured!
And all the while, our Lord He cajoles.

The price remains the same for all time.
Christ promised us that he'd bank our place,
With the Trinity, where they embrace,
Those of us proclaiming faith sublime.

Your CD will renew when due
And interest earned is your loving Christ,
For your sins and future, He sacrificed.
—Daily re-bonding, we're born anew.

—Bill Greene 12Oct 2008

SIGN LANGUAGE OF LOVE

That kiss from across the room says
What you feel and what you know,
That offering love helps you grow,
Like you are sending sweet bouquets.

A soft touch that's held for a while,
Or a warm meeting with her eyes,
Can inspire a heartbeat to rise,
Which in time sweeps her down the aisle.

Chocolates work, Valentines too,
To earn a preferred place in her heart.
F'Heaven's sake, sometime it should start!
—To meld two, into one milieu.

An Aisle trip is a blessed one,
Leading to honors by the Lord,
Committing to keep Him aboard,
So your accounts there won't overrun.

—Billy Cornflake 1-11-09

CARING FAMILIES

In Jesus name, caring families shine,
As I pray that they are yours and mine.
As our breathing acts without a prompt
One's love in action is paramount.

Spontaneously our hearts respond
For this love is way beyond fond.
Thoughtfulness inspires ways to support
So peacefulness attends one's comport.

No matter the cause of distresses
Some gentleness and caresses,
So often will soften a concern,
Enabling a welcome U-turn.

Better still is long term commitment,
As to Christ even today in Lent.
That we apply in prescient presence,
Modeled by His love so immense.

The Philos kind toward our fellow man,
God love

—William F. Greene 2-1-09

WORK INSIDE?

Starts with happiness,
Warmed by a caress,
Cranking one's motor,
What a promoter!

While that works just fine,
It makes outside divine,
With a smile and "Hello",
'Til others feel mello.

"Nice work" I would say,
Loving self on display
And others as well,
As Christ rings one's bell.

—A playful Billy Cornflake 2-16-10

AUTUMN LEAVES

Orange, yellows and browns of trees,
Arrive each Fall for us to please.
Fall attire in each of those hues,
From which we may choose and amuse.

We'd rake leaves in a knee deep pile,
For romping fun so versatile.
A blaze then would so vaporize,
Those early Autumn times our prize.

A favorite season is this,
For many who will reminisce,
When shared relationships blossom,
Wholesome as in a David's Psalm.

Autumn leaves us and then moves on,
Like Sandberg's Fog and your Leprechaun,
While colorfully we seek Him,
In deepening faith, more than whim.

—Billy Cornflake, Lay Pastor,
1ˢᵗ UMC, Lompoc, CA 9-25-2010

AW SHUCKS!

Giving thanks is hard to do,
Though it's rarely a boo boo.
Mannered people give thanks well,
And it softens a hard shell.
So expressing gratitude
Represents that you're not rude.

—Billy Cornflake 6Nov96

FAIRER STILL

Three shades of love,
To celebrate
This Day St.Valentine
Bequeathed.

Objectively,
They make one whole,
With love committed
Deep in the soul.

Eros surely,
Warms blood, desire.
Philos too,
Denies the ire.

Yet, Agape,
Modeled by our Lord,
Transcends each other hue:
Love's grandest award.

One striving toward
Such Lord-like love,
Humbly offers self and spirit,
For eternity.

– William F. Greene 1-19-00

TO A SINGLE MOM

How to atone,
When you're alone . . .
The struggle to keep
Young ones safe and well
Is one painful story to tell.

Singleness by any cause,
At times softened by
Grandpas and grandmas,
Promotes your womanpower,
Needed daily hour by hour.

I tip my hat and honor thee
For meeting responsibility.
As plans and schedules collide
You still find means to
stem their tide.
Looking inward saved the day,
When it seemed like hell to pay.

My mom like you
With four to shoe,
Networked like mad
When times were bad.
She looked outward
In a model A Ford
To family and neighbors
And lots of her Lord.

So even alone, others care,
Understand and will share.
Love anew in many forms,
Warms hearts, little ones too,
Enabling wise moms to renew.
Bless you as you strive and heal,
Wearing a smile with soft appeal.

—9May2000 W.F. Greene, (who raised 4 solo.)

MORE THAN FRIENDS

An extraordinary Friend
To revere and treasure,
Respect yes, even love,
Sharing depths and pleasure.

Such high regard, no whim
And rarest to our being,
Immersed in soul and spirit.
As one believes in Him.

—William F. Greene 1-17-00

MOTHERS STYLE

Often when we're grown and alone,
Her tender touch and patient ear,
Influence us throughout our lives
And works for us throughout our years.

Teacher-mentor to all of us,
Seldom harsh, firm when needed,
Her calm leadership's at its best
And helpful where its roots she seeded.

Thank you Mothers, I pray we've learned,
To honor truth and tolerance.
Slow to anger-quick to forgive,
And keep a happy countenance!

A loved son—William F. Greene 1May2001

F' HEAVEN'S SAKE!

A "March of Times" before our eyes,
By chance can lead to paradise.
No matter how that past unfolds,
Ahead, there'll be some new thresholds.
Careers, mating, interests galore,
How to choose from those in store?

That's where Jesus comes in to play,
Perhaps not sought just yesterday.
Free will and conscience stir the heart,
"Shall I or not His will impart?"
From there, it's the path we take,
So let it be for "Heaven's Sake!"

—Bill Greene 2-20-07

DEAR FRIENDS

Sending to you a version of my heart,
Sets Valentine's Day off to a fine start.
What the heart contains surely tells it all,
Not Billy Cornflake's usual tale tall!

It is instead mindfulness of dear friends,
Who over time gave me big dividends.
So it is my way to say, "Thank You" very much,
For continuing to remain in touch!

Memories shared, show in some picture frames,
Hopefully noting both the time and names,
So in our later years we can say "Yes,
Weren't those days of great happiness"!
Warmly sent,

—Bill Greene 2-14-09

CHRISTMAS POEMS
CONTENTS

A CHRISTMAS REFLECTION

At Christmastime we all will know,
how grand it is to give and glow.
Others in the world know woe:
for them, the extra mile we'll go.

Dear friends and family do grow,
because we pray and love them so.
Tradition says the Babe did show,
yet 'member Mary and St. Joe!

—Merry Christmas! Dec 1988

HO HO

What'll we do this Christmas season.
For kids I guess we'll be appeasin'.
Oh, His birthday means much more than that,
So why not have a fireside chat?

Suppose we inventory feelings:
Positives that will paint the ceilings
And other ones too that yule suppress,
Or better yet—to grant forgiveness!

Now a Christmas plan can be carefree.
Of course there will be a shopping spree.
"Take good care of family and friends
And the needy for big dividends."

Then a quiet time so that yule find
Solace in a relaxed state of mind.
A softer view of life here on earth,
That will make it fun to spread some mirth . . .

—William F. Greene 11-13-91

MINNESOTA CHRISTMAS 1991

"Fa la la la la, la la la la"
Christmas for Kendra and Con-Tessa!
Bright eyes and believers are all around.
When Santa comes, they won't make a sound.
Now they're all glad they did as they should!
Expectations fulfilled feel so good.
Yes, children at Christmas do perk things up,
'Specially while they are filling their cup.
Enjoy yourselves as never before
And remember those who need it more . . .

—Santa flake 25 December 1991

HEAVENLY GIFTS

Each Christmas child in this world
needs our help as life's unfurled.
Children need environment
safe with lots of sentiment.
Stimulate dreams and desire
and decency they require.
With encouragement, not fear,
all these youngsters will endear.

—William F. Greene 11-5-92

THOUGHTS OF CHILDREN
AT CHRISTMAS

Christmas is just right for kids.
Toys pile up like pyramids.
Know that giving means our love,
for all of you are well thought of.
We pray you will play and live
and learn that you can forgive.
Ah—the name of Christ child's game
a trait for which one can aim . . .

—William F. Greene 11-8-92

TINSEL '94

Christmas wishes in rhyming lines
Are all because the east star shines.
With gifts we celebrate as then
While hoping He will come again.

The praises we sing lift hearts high
To Him who became a Rabbi.
Our Christian roots are deep and firm
Which we can now in joy confirm.

And so Merry Christmas to all
With or without any snowfall!

—William F. Greene 9Dec94

PLEASE, LORD:

This Christmas perhaps we could pray
For soldiers out Bosnia way.
Forgiving ancient enemies,
Especially in this winter's freeze,
Is our true hope for Balkan folk,
Then peace will be a masterstroke.

With that accord our boys can be
Rewarded there with ennui.
And loved ones at home spared the grief
To overjoy beyond belief,
When Johnny marches home to stay,
For him we do fervently pray.

—William F. Greene 12-6-95

HOLIDAY FRAGRANCE

All through the house into my nose,
As I sit in this writing pose,
Bringing memories of way back when
—Christmas goodies in the oven.

Visions of sugar plums begin,
Laughter and surprises within,
From Christmases past, a montage
—My very personal mirage . . .

Sight, sound and fragrance remind
Of happy family ties that bind.
I'll tell it now and be concise,
There's nothing like holiday spice!

—Billy Cornflake 12-2-92 Santa's Village

A 2ND MILLENIUM

JOY TO THE WORLD

Let love prevail this Christmastide,
His peacefulness in us abide.
As each gift's placed beneath a tree,
Recall Three Wise Men's jubilee!

—William F. Greene 12-12-99

WASSAIL

Holidays come lightning fast,
'Specially at this time of year.
So pause a bit, feel good cheer,
As Santa's being quite typecast.

'Tis time for lots of sentiment,
With people we care for most,
To dear friendships, lift a toast!
They're the grandest ornament!

Some come visit from afar,
From across the continent,
Or an ocean in torment,
To reach their bright
Twinkling star.

—William F. Greene 12-12-99

A WINTER BIRTHDAY

Christmas feelings
warm the heart,
Sharing, family, with love,
While a star shines high above
—The Christ child
was there to start.
Add-ons to that early theme,
Embrace gifting to supplant
Caroling as we incant,
A Child we feel is supreme . . .
In giving and receiving,
Can we perceive in a sense
Because of His innocence)
A gift represents the King?

—Bill Greene, Dec2000

ON CHRISTMAS 2001

To pause awhile for the Christ Child
Strengthens us to pursue boldly,
Virtue in His fine example,
For dreams and ambitions self-styled.

In this tragic year especially,
We need His grace to proceed,
With relentless faith and conviction,
To embrace again, life peacefully.

We pray for you and humanity,
To firm our goals joyfully
And share with us your calm,
With love, our mutual warrantee.

—Bill & Marion Greene

TO HONOR JESUS BIRTH

His son with crown, a diadem,
An heir to David in Bethlehem,
Pronounced at an angel's behest,
Lo, incarnation manifest!

One carpenter's son of Virgin birth,
Who in 30 years would prove his worth.
We humbly pray in adoration,
Within this freedom loving nation.

And with joyous humility,
Honoring Christ's nativity,
Mindful of His great compassion,
Enhanced again by resurrection.

We Pray that someday our world will please
Our God who made all this with ease.
When each with shoulder to the wheel
Can help make peace and charity real.

—Bill Greene 21Nov 2002

A CHRISTIAN CONCERN

Little tippy-toes with turned up nose,
Our young gather 'round him we suppose.
Their simple belief in goodness of man,
Ignores those weaknesses he's better than.

Those who risk theirs to save another's skin,
The package is saved, but what is within?
That red-suited ideal appeals to most,
A kid who doesn't, his Christmas is toast!

A fairyland view of Santa Claus fame,
Creatively extols his well known name.
Does it replace the Lad from a manger?
For some, yes, but to more, He's no stranger!

We enjoy the pageantry, even myth,
Caroling graces—created by songsmith,
Confusing faith with myth, being self-styled.
Still, closer we strive to know the Christ Child.

He is the rock, higher than I . . . Borrowed from Ps. 61

Merry Christmas,
—Bill Greene Dec. 2003

"HERE I AM"

In uplifting times
Since Jesus birth,
The Star of Bethlehem
Shone "Here I am".

And so He, alive with love,
Guides us both then and now,
While all we need do
Is to live His vow.

That little Babe
Soon changed our world
With a simple message
Faith hope and love;

His Agape embraces us all
Then Eros was given to enflame,
So our love of fellow man.
Is what Philos became.

As we elevate each heart and mind
Toward the Christ child kind and pure
Rededicate in faith, hope and love
In Him with whom we are secure.

Merry Christmas!
—Bill Greene 2004

WELCOME BABY JESUS

Advent holy time warms our hearts,
With the love Jesus name imparts.
Enough to share with those we know,
Even square dance to Dozey Do!

Lighten up in this Christmas time,
Raising your spirits to sublime,
Smiling much more than ever may,
Hint at how much for those we pray.
Jesus,
Each year you bring us mem'ries grand,
And lots of love we understand.
Welcome to your World, Jesus child,
Where you were here once domiciled.
Love the baby Jesus!

—Bill Greene 5Dec 2009

REJOICE ON CHRISTMAS

Our Christmas music says so much to us,
With décor, Jesus and our gifts a plus.
It's only sad when it's time moves on –
So let's enjoy our Christmas marathon!

—Bill Greene 10 Dec 2010

ALASKA POEMS CONTENTS

William F. Greene
17September 1995

Friends,

You asked for some poems that I wrote,
some were ashore, others afloat.
Tongue in cheek you'll find is there,
but also truth, written with care.
Conceived quickly, I hope they're sweet
and that you'll find a few are neat.

These were written on the Princess Cruise and tours
of the Yukon and Alaska from Vancouver, B.C.
to Anchorage, AK from 2-13Sept 1995.

THE GOOD SHIP SKY PRINCESS

There are some who will take a cruise
for the good times with things to choose,
While others in the weight room will
do aerobics to get their fill.

In between the casino lures
as long as one's wallet endures.
Ice cream time brings out all us kids
from bridge games having made some bids.

Walks around open decks entreat,
with some romance, they can't be beat.
New friends are made at dinner time,
part of the cruise that's so sublime.

Putting but no golf ball driving
was all there was for macho striving.
Attendants at one's elbow can
execute any whim you plan.

Entertainers, both day and night
parade in costumes naughty tight.
There is no vapor trail at sea,
who cares, when there's you'n me!

—Billy Cornflake 3Sept.1995

ALONG THE WP & YR RR

At first men thought that it would fail,
the White Pass and Yukon Route Rail.
Yet in two years from south and north
frozen dynamiters held forth.
While the Klondike Gold Rush had ended,
that Whitehorse link to sea tended
for growing commerce with Yukon
that west Canada would grow on.

First with steam then diesel would come,
disappointing railroaders some.
Tourists now rise 3,000 feet
through granite cliffs that are a treat . . .
Aspen, Poplar, Spruce 'n Maple,
grow to heights that astound people.
Rugged peaks with glacier between
create quite a dramatic scene.

Most of this in one brief hour
with frequently a flower bower.
Chilkoot Pass Trail, a few feet wide,
where the weaker prospectors died,
carved there by wear of men and their mules,
who carried provisions and tools.
We can only commiserate
on their hazards and forlorn fate.

Honesty, a measure of man,
sort out those who also ran.
Some found gold to lose to a thief,
'til mounties law gave some relief.
Miners would share all that they had
as they mixed among the good and bad.
Times would change, but people would not,
when challenged, we give all that we've got!

—William F. Greene 5Sept.1995

FRONTIER'S INN

A wildlife museum life-like scene
—Canadian animals pristine,
recreated taxidermy style,
from tundra wolf to ptarmigan guile,
demonstrated nature's own refrain,
where each of them fits in the food chain.
Grizzlies, black, brown and polar bears white
made for us a magnificent sight.
Owls, hawks and an artic black rat,
even a lynx and mountain lion cat,
with billy goat ram and mountain sheep,
next to caribou and elk that keep,
a careful watch over duck and goose,
in case some predator's on the loose.
Artful works, interestingly displayed,
a nice treat on our Yukon parade.

—William F. Greene 5Sept.1995

DAWSON CITY IN BLOOM

Dancing girls with backfield in motion
are apt to give some guys a notion.
Naughty, naughty if one's wife's nearby,
unless he sneaks a peek on the sly!

—Billy Cornflake 7Sept. 1995

SHOW TIME

Watching others panning gold,
shows the fever's mighty old.
'Forty-niners had it first,
an insatiable gold thirst.
Sourdoughs in 'ninety-eight,
bound for gold, couldn't wait.
Gold's appeal in every time
captures heartbeats, rings a chime.
Guys and gals still prospecting
for any kind they're panning.
Golden Girls in golden years,
keeps us smiling with upbeat cheers.
Charlatans will take your dough,
for gold we're told, "they ain't no mo"!

—Billy Cornflake 9Sept.1995

THE BLOSSOMING OF DAWSON CITY

The Eldorado, just five feet wide
was where they would find the gold trail hide.
Nearby was the Discovery Claim
which became known in fortune and fame,
found by Carmack on Bonanza Creek,
signaling others within a week.
Dawson City, better known on maps
attracted many thousands of chaps.
Placer gold taken from nearby streams
answered some of those prospectors dreams.
Soon the easy gold was mostly gleaned,
then dredgers came for the finely screened.
Today, tourism is the miners "trade"
there in Dawson City, where we stayed.
Local people who live there year-round
are pleased because gangs do not abound.
Traffic lights are absent in their town
where unpaved streets offer some renown.
Why did we all come? Mystique, I guess,
and couldn't settle for any less.
A mine night foreman we met that day
told us with vigor just why he'd stay.
Hard skills developed throughout his years
sustained him and we offered our cheers!

—William F. Greene 8Sept. 1995

MIDNIGHT SUN EXPRESS

By rail from Fairbanks to Denali
in a lush green and verdant valley,
breakfast was served in style below,
while later above under glass dome
we bumped and jostled when we'd roam.
Rather chummy, we'd call this ride
pairs faced pairs, bondings abide.
Bright aspen gold challenged black spruce,
roots intertwined and weren't loose.
We passed mountains and canyon dead-ends,
streams and lakes clear or gray glacier sends.
Infrequently, Mt. McKinley rose
out of self-made mist and repose.
This comfy four hour ride would end,
but Denali's our dividend!

—Billy Cornflake 9Sept.1995

MATT TAYLOR'S LAST DRIVE

From Yukon's narrow gauge railway,
To Fairbanks, his home, Matt held sway.
Three days he was great company.
Up affably, incredibly.
A night in Sam Mc Gee's Whitehorse,
with his cremation, some remorse.
On to Dawson City's gold mines
with dancing girls in barroom shrines.

In fog out of Dawson City,
we were somber and not witty.
"Top o' the World" a barren place,
wind 'n weather come face to face.
The few trees there are short and lean,
with brush that's yellow red 'n green.
Permafrost twelve inches below
permits just shallow roots to grow.

From Alcan to Dawson City,
an unpaved road is quite gritty.
Poker Creek, population 2,
a U.S. Border Crossing Crew
at just over four thousand feet,
few people and no where to eat.
We traveled light, just juice 'n fruit
but wore a trusty union suit.

Busing down along Jack Wade Creek,
more trees appeared where're we'd peek,
but miners had dredged gold dust thin,
leaving stone piles where they had been.
A Dodge pickup with trailer towed
played "chicken" with us on that road.
Valley surveyors, a surprise
were using sights for their sore eyes.

Chicken, Alaska came in view,
and we would pause, not just pass through.
A cafe, bar and liquor store,
with gift shop for those who craved more.
"Chicken" becomes ptarmigan stew,
seems to be the right thing to do.
A white mountain goat Marion saw,
where shooting is agin' the law.

His summer job with Princess Cruise
demands much and he's paid his dues.
Our master degreed driver Matt,
traffic undaunted, still would chat
good humouredly on stark terrain
that with knowledge he could explain.
A road crew stopped us at their whim,
so Matt showed an Aurora film.

148

The Caterpillar graders there
were making the road wider with care.
Middle clouds broke for sun to shine
on us below, far from the brine.
The angels seldom visit here
among the caribou 'n deer.
Good lunch at Tok produced broad smiles,
with ahead easy Alcan miles.

The Mentasta Range heading west,
shielded mountain goats near its crests.
Those snow capped Alaska Range tops
make very exciting back-drops.
Rika's Roadhouse, a sale of sales,
Is where tourist business long prevails.
So Matt, thank you from way down deep
our memories with you we'll long keep!

—William F. Greene 8Sept.1995

ANAHEE

In Fairbanks, Alaska afloat,
Discovery III, a river boat
hosted our tour and some others,
mostly granddads and grandmothers.
Before we left the cozy dock,
a Cessna float plane with a shock,
took-off alongside of us there,
before most of us were aware.
Anahee, it seemed here applied,
meaning "hurry-up" I confide.
That Anthabascan term we'd learn,
to move on, not be left astern.
Yupik Tribe Mike Angiak would
be a teacher, best that he could.

An example of how they're blest,
native Alaskans at their best
educated, return back home
instead of running off to roam.
Mike, graduate of Notre Dame
is now in Fairbanks with more flame
to pay his people back who gave
the opportunity he'd crave.
Alicia's in third college year
will also have a like career.
Alaska born, our driver Matt,
Boston C. proletariat,
grooms retarded children with love
from whence he came, Fairbanks thereof.

A Piper Cub took off ashore,
landing on the same spot as before.
We could see that flying made sense,
along Chena River immense.
A river boat Captain was there,
of his 55 years he'd share.
Iditatrod's Susan Butcher,
with hubby, lived on that river,
breeding huskies for that long race,
who romped for us with happy face.
Yonder in that early morn light,
Mt. McKinley was in our sight.
and that is noteworthy because
it's seldom seen, often withdraws.
On the left bank, a salmon trap
turned slowly aiming to kidnap
an eager fish, swimming upstream
hoping to reach its breeding dream.

An Indian mother and child,
showed smoking salmon in the wild.
The Anthabaskan camp was there,
with skins of caribou 'n hare.
Alicia Dozette of that tribe
was on hand and she would describe
living in their huts weatherproof
or in framed building with turf roof.
Discovery III's whistle blew,
so "anahee" was what we'd do!

—William F. Greene 9Sept.1995

DENALI ENTREATS

By school bus through Denali Park,
from just after noon until dark,
we rolled and scanned for the wild game,
like bears we are told are not tame.
Driver Laughton's vision ahead
spoke of bear and eagles wingspread.
Someone spotted a caribou,
munching brush we could not see through.
In a while, Dall ewe and lambs white
were ridge high and beyond wolf's fright.
Soon grizzlies appeared, up high too,
the mom 'n three cubs derring do,
frolicking in a berry patch,
no predator would be a match.

Mt. McKinley, seen through some clouds
fifty miles west, above the crowds,
snow draped and nearly four miles high,
"The big one" Indians decry.
That's what Denali means, we're told
its volcanic granite's quite old.
Nostalgia aside, one fox red
hunted so that he would be fed.
More sheep and bear, often it seemed
brought us peering when someone screamed.
Two more caribou, ten-point bucks
foraged confident like Mack trucks.
That bald eagle near a ridge line
soared in search of a meal divine,
with motionless wing, rising air
made him appear quite debonaire.
At rest stops, we'd view jagged peaks,
some as sharp as predators beaks.

The driver stopped, a falcon flew,
gracefully until out of view.
No wolf pack ever crossed our trail,
they were searching for something frail.
While we relaxed, after six hours,
admiring some natures flowers,
a road block ahead of RVs,
foretold a treat, bull moose would please.
Their shoulder height was much higher
than others found in wooded briar.
Then their massive antlers were seen,
feasting on willow so serene,
fearless as caribou before,
majestic beasts, wanting no war.

In our bus, excitement roared,
Richard's stroke left us feeling gored.
Skilled care respond to his side,
and now in Fairbanks, he does reside.
We pray for Richard and his wife
for good health and a happy life.

The weather was mild, driver skilled,
our satisfaction was fulfilled.

—William F. Greene 9Sept.1995

AURORA BOREALIS

Harbor lights from north on high,
make one spectacular sky.
Endlessly in amorphous forms,
colors in vivid dancing swarms,
with ions that our sun controls
captured near earth's magnetic poles
dance as their energy turns light
in their infinite glory bright.
Some harm is brought but never meant
to what we call our firmament.
Otherwise that creator's gift
seems an intended swift uplift.

—Billy Cornflake 9Sept.1995

ANCHORAGE SUNRISE
IN THE WEST!

From the Sheraton's fourteenth floor,
we saw some of nature's splendor:
low clouds over Prince William Sound,
to the horizon all around
except for opening to the west
over a northwest mountain crest.
The unseen sunrise from the east
reached west between cloud layers and pleased
to glow against a pocket where
it made us feel the sun was there!

—Billy Cornflake 11Sept.1995

FROM DENALI TO ANCHORAGE

Alaska Rail to Anchorage,
would take all day and did engage.
Along the River Nenana part way,
in valley's broad splendid array,
red sockeye salmon struggled to
their place of birth for a clue.
Alaskans live near this rail line,
for good reason, that's their design.
The tiny villages there though
are for survival and not show.
Distant mountain ranges reveal
the Pacific plate movement's real
Many a shallow pond we'd see,
above frost with nary a tree.
For us the dinner bell rang late
and prime rib is what we two ate.
Alaskans have this way to go,
in wilderness they won't outgrow.

—Billy Cornflake 10Sept.1995

NOT CATALINA ISLE

Twenty-six miles across the sound,
crashing down glaciers will be found,
like advancing soldiers so bold,
with few if any growing old.
Progressing glaciers come to rest,
reaching oceans their final test.
Geological wonders they,
forming valleys once covered clay,
leaving rocks, gravel and debris
endless labor, glacier ennui!

—Billy Cornflake 11Sept.1995

HAVE YOU HEARD?

Start with humor, not a rumor
and thereby miss all the uproar.
Very simply put, a chuckle will
fill voids a rumor never will.
For humor's known to be just that,
tossing rumor in a cocked hat.

—William F. Greene 3Sept.1995

A GLACIER TALE

Unable to steam in College Fiord,
for fog in there had too far lowered,
so on we went to Barry instead,
where the Cascade and Coxe Glaciers shed.
Gingerly we neared an icy cliff,
where folks outside were frozen stiff.
We waited close by but all that we got,
was some ice cracking like a shot.
shutterbugs photographed each other,
they'd traveled too far not to bother.
Drizzle and chill would bring us all in,
where hot chocolate and such weren't sin.
Our Aussie catamaran sailed well
in Prince William Sound so gentle swell.
The crew were open, helpful and kind
and fed us well, seeming not to mind.
More glaciers we'd view, waterfalls too,
while peering for eagles that were few.
Videos of Alaska and ice,
would help us all to remember twice.
The expert master kept our cruise safe,
avoiding most of the ice floe chafe.
This long day we will remember well
and you can bet our friends we will tell!

—Billy Cornflake 11Sept.1995

BACK TO BASICS

Working men we meet and have known
grow quite tall and stand on their own.
No more perfect than you or me,
but shoulder loads naturally.
The physical and macho guys
can easily attract gals eyes,
while others draw less attention,
they're part of the same convention.
Honest, skilled and dedicated,
salt o' the earth Lord created.
Flexible too, when layoffs come
and smartly they have saved up some.
Gummint says "I am here to help",
but all his tax man does is yelp.
People solve problems, gummint can't,
lower taxes, reduce the grant.
In case they haven't got it yet,
isn't it time to lower debt?

—William F.Greene 4Sept.1995

WHISTLE 'ROUND THE BEND

On steam driven trains in olden days,
the crew were revered in many ways.
Friendly conductors kept us informed,
always cheery and black uniformed.
Brakemen in coveralls and corncob pipe,
ran over freight cars without a gripe
and always ready to slow her when,
the train downhill speed went up again.
Engineers who whistled in striped cap,
were not known ever to take a nap
and would always wave, coming through town
'cause we'd return it without a frown.
Firemen, though shoveled coal all the while
and we wondered if they could smile.
The mail car-another mystery,
did they anticipate robbery?
Ah, we say of those times long ago,
"Lucky trainmen, traveling to 'n fro,
what a wonderful life that would be,
new faces 'n places, yessiree!"

—Billy Cornflake 8Sept.1995

WHAT IT TAKES

Temptation that can control,
is just fine if it's a goal,
one worthy of your striving,
dedication and heartstring.

—Billy Cornflake 10Sept.1995

MUTUTALITY

Mesmerized and tantalized,
I am by your dancing eyes.
eyes that say things that eye like
"come closer, don't take a hike."

—Billy Cornflake 4Sept.1995

ON SPIRITS

Spirit thrives in many a form,
mixing them could be the norm.
Those external and some within
do combine to create a win,
amounting to one's synergy,
created with one's own energy.
Networking with self starter zeal
has for some a strong appeal,
so helping self achieve a goal
will pay off and not take a toll.
God-like spirits many faces,
and are known to provide graces.
When that spirit resides inside
it can result in lasting pride.
Enthusiastically pursued,
objectives are reached by the shrewd.
So spirited spirit makes sense,
for an outcome that is immense!

—William F. Greene 5Sept.1995

MEDITATION

Reflections look at you left and right.
A mirror in front and one behind,
look in either and you will find,
they copy each other out of sight.

It doesn't matter what's else in view,
only the way each mirror is placed,
determines how reflections are traced,
though smaller, each succeeding view's true.

Reflections reach out and some can haunt,
something out of the long dismal past,
when others might have been in the cast,
and that outreach can be a taunt.

Reflections of good times may dispel
anxieties long buried away,
when all the while you would hope and pray
that old reflection would soon farewell.

Whatever it was that tinged us so,
can we learn how to shed the lament
whether shame or embarrassment
and restore more of our inner glow.

—Billy Cornflake 8Sept.1995

THE HIGH ROAD

Doers are those who make living neat,
grass doesn't grow beneath busy feet.
As much for oneself, do for others,
that will makes all of them one's brothers.
Lay off the cigarettes and booze
and make your life a smoother cruise.
And when happiness replaces blame,
one's anger will wallow in its shame.
All the while in the universe,
listen and when talking, be terse.

—Billy Cornflowers 7Sept.1995

MOVING ON

Mighty thunder would telegraph
A glacier's death and epitaph.
Then breaking off and crashing down
Into Prince William Sound renown,
For ice floes, sea otters and their pups
Nurtured by their loving grown-ups.
That glacier face, a hundred feet high
Would soon break off to be small fry.
End of the trail, blue ice 'n white,
If caught off guard, it might cause fright.
Beautiful though, in its last hour,
Nudged endlessly by glacier power.
It won't stop when earth warming ends
For then a new ice age transcends!

—William F. Greene Written and

read with Captain's permission
on a 100 passenger Trimaran
in Prince William Sound
Sept 11,1995

VERMONT POEMS 2001
CONTENTS

TWILIGHT IN VERMONT

(All VT by Billy Cornflake in June 2001)

A hazy new moon as June bugs flash,
Betrayed the red fox cross-meadow dash.
At ten P.M., birds nesting high,
Regenerating from a long day's fly.

No sound at all-except brook side,
Where stillness watched as the trout hide.
Summer in Vermont is warm,
Yet not many mosquitoes swarm.

Traffic is much less at this hour,
Adding to the solace power,
Meditating's easy you know,
My mind's at rest, warm feelings flow.

A SILENT BIRD FEEDER

A lady finch pecks at the feeder.
A young grey squirrel looks on-wondering.
He climbs down a porch rail to fallen seed,
Then gracefully on his haunches, feed.

A bright yellow male finch joins the scene,
to munch, then to himself preen.
A wonder is that they learn so well,
How could that silent feeder tell?

SERIOUSLY

As some trees rise above others,
So too are those who must achieve,
Find and use an inner power,
Beyond what many can conceive.

Such dramatic power, Lord driven
Surpassing an unfounded plan,
Energizes the soul and mind,
And has ever since time began.

TREASURE IN CHESTER, VERMONT

Baba a' Louis Bakery
Built where a stately farmhouse burned
Makes pastry, bread, quiche and coffee,
Satisfying palates tastefully.

Gabled but otherwise un-Vermont,
Roof beams curve to find the earth,
So interior's open wide.,
Baking behind, food served up-front.

Designed well outside and in,
slant-curved windows the entry adorn,
Suggesting height inside to see,
Then hand-crafted dining tables within.

South facing windows, reveal submerged
A garden once farm basement there.
Where ladies groups tea-luncheon with flair,
While we linger over noon fare served.

Inspired are we, like when vows renewed,
With delightful intimacy,
Over shared lives revered, we recommit,
This well bonded love since before we wed.

FREEDOMS: FROM AND FOR

Freedom from oppression provides,
Choices that each person decides:
For hedonists at one extreme,
To philanthropists with a dream.

While some betwixt may neither be;
Their main harm is internally,
Set apart from worldly care,
Perhaps of duty they're unaware.

Alexandr Solzhenitsyn
Said Freedom "FOR" if not now, when?
Yet his plea has gone unheeded,
By those who sense they weren't needed.

St. Paul preached, "Abandon Law,
Just love and hold the Lord in awe".
That's a start as you will see,
Leading the righteous heavenly.

Responsibility is the key,
To enable society.
A Christian Nation standing tall,
By example and just like Paul.

He knew the spirit within him
Would sustain when times were grim.
Prisons could not stop his work,
To spread Christ's word to Greek and Turk.

As individual Christians we,
Can define our own destiny.
What shall it be, as Paul has done
—or lead a life that's aimed at fun?

That choice is ours in Freedoms FOR,
So in choosing may we explore,
What talents have we to provide,
Services that need be applied.

Like teaching men then how to fish
—got them moving, not merely wish.
While motivation thrives within,
A caring nudge can help one win!

SEAMLESSLY

Vermont has a way
to soften one's mood.
In a few days, it's peacefulness,
creeps in
while time slows to a crawl.
Its most verdant forest and meadow,
green mountain and brook,
sparkle while driving past,
slowly of course,
(fifty is mighty fast!)
Birds, deer and small mammals
punctuate scenes.
—What's happening all this while,
Is the beauty within one's soul
meets its mate in nature,
to coalesce, seamlessly,
so one is unaware that its grandeur
has performed a makeover in you
of what you really are.
Transcendental?

TURTLING

Some time away from routine care,
Has made us two very aware,
Of things more important to us,
Like listening, for one—such a plus.

Early rise or not—what the heck,
For whom will ever care to check?
Timing actions by week or day,
Allows for more of carefree play.

We'll see how well this lesson's learned,
When we're at home, IF less concerned!
Remembering when we are there,
The gentleness we've longed to share.

MID-WEST FROM ALOFT

Those acres down there,
With produce and the dairy man,
Some green, others tan,
Show well the farmers care.

If problems are known
In agrarian land,
From 40,000 feet, they seem bland
And thank them for seed they've sown.

Some cumulus clouds beyond the wing,
Look tame, with no 'build-ups' or rain.
Blue sky above and clear ahead,
Snug in seatbelt, to a novel I cling.

WARMLY GIVEN

A two hundred twelve year-old farmhouse.
A cold front passing, brisk wind blows.
Built to resist Vermont snows, timbers creak.
Near fields with deer, foxes and grouse.

Charm is part of what this place means,
Wood is tastefully blended with care.
Welcome is the warmth I declare,
Of memories drawn from our hosts genes.

The lively dialogue we share,
Stimulates and engages minds,
As friends enhance a tie that binds,
Fulfillment of sorts, to be fair.

If home is where one finds the heart,
This home has heart, one will reflect,
Courtesy, humor, intellect
And joyfully it does impart.

WHIMSY

Our gentle hosts, cousin Pat'n Phil,
Drove to a picnic site on a rise,
Some 50 feet above where waters flowed,
And nature's wonders pleased our eyes.

Would Deer slayer emerge to find
Intruders in his virgin land,
Or greet us with a friendly hand,
Even join-in to learn we're kind?

That wisp of fancy vaporized,
As playfully that stream I named,
"*Shields Brook*", no one could decode,
Yet humor would not be denied!

LOFTY VIEW

An elevated porch railing,
A meadowlark's love song.
The property line vertical steles,
Maples and elm frame the sight.

Lawn mowed in places,
Wild flowers beyond—reach
To the brook bank where
Nourished, more maples thrive.

Those pastel hollyhocks stretch high
Toward a tall bird house
Invitingly there
With entries too small for jays and crows

Lifting my serene gaze,
A tree crested knoll
Fills the panorama
Of this calm Vermont scene.

A tenacious male jay,
Assaults a small bird feeder, fruitlessly
And flies away in noisy contempt.
His mate pecks a few seeds tho'.

Before me
The open white French Door,
Framed by maple-stained,
Invites one to venture
Onto the porch deck
In misty morn coolness.

Behind and above me
In a colonial rocker
The bunk-loft for kids
Deepens a sense of awe
This Chester farmhouse inspires.

Ah, the morning coffee brews,
It's aromatics wafting toward me,
As anticipation interrupts a soleful mood
And contentment fulfills sip by sip.

—Uncle Billy Cornflake, Chester, VT 15 June 2001